HUMMINGBIRDS

HUMMINGBIRDS

Dorset Press
New York

A QUINTET BOOK

This edition published 1989 by Dorset Press,
a division of Marboro Books Corporation,
ISBN 0– 88029–368–3

This book was designed and produced by
Quintet Publishing Limited
6 Blundell Street
London N7 9BH

Creative Director: Peter Bridgewater
Designer: Terry Jeavons
Project Editor: Shaun Barrington
Editor: James McCarter

Typeset in Great Britain by
Central Southern Typesetters, Eastbourne
Manufactured in Hong Kong by Regent Publishing
Services Limited
Printed in Hong Kong by Leefung-Asco Printers
Limited

PICTURE CREDITS

FOREWORD
DR NOBLE PROCTOR

....

The ten-year-old boy stretched as far as he could from the top of the stone wall and gently bent the limb slowly downward. On the limb, looking like a lichen-covered knot, was the nest of a Ruby-throated Hummingbird and within, a precious treasure – two pea-sized eggs! That ten-year-old was myself and it was my first experience with a hummingbird. That fascination has continued over the years and has led me in pursuit of these feathered gems throughout the New World, from the edge of the snowfields in the Andes to the dark bamboo thickets of the Amazon Basin. I have not been alone. Early literature indicates an abiding fascination with hummingbirds; these tiny packages that seem to exude the very essence of life are one of the most celebrated of all bird groups.

Hummingbirds are found only in the New World but have a very extensive range. The Northern limit of the group is Southern Canada and the lower portion of Alaska. To the South hummingbirds are found right down in the windswept, mountainous areas of Tierra del Fuego at the extreme southern tip of the continent. Within that extensive range over 320 species form the family Trochilidae. Their names, nearly as alluring as the birds themselves, entice the birder to conjure up visions of what the birds might look like: evocative, colorful names like Glowing Puffleg, Amethyst Throated Sungem, Booted Racquet Tail, Plovercrest and Crested Coquette. At the extremes of their range few species can be found but as one approaches the Equator the numbers increase dramatically. Well over 50 species are represented in the small Central American country of Costa Rica alone.

Many species spend most of their life in a restricted area. Others undergo limited migrational movement that may be as simplistic as an altitudinal change in a mountain range or as dramatic as intercontinental movement that will see them cover thousands of miles. The Rufous Hummingbird may make a journey that will carry it from Southern Alaska to the forests of Nicaragua. Its Eastern counterpart, the Ruby-throated Hummingbird sometimes journeys from Southern Canada to Panama, including the breathtaking non-stop journey of 500 miles across the Gulf of Mexico, en route to its final wintering area. Quite a feat for a bird weighing no more than two or three grams!

Their brilliant plumage is enough in itself to motivate many people to study them and attempt to lure them to feeding stations for closer scrutiny: a shimmering iridescence found nowhere else in the birdworld, set off by outlandish head plumes, spectacular gorgets and extreme modifications of the tail. Size runs the gamut from the 2½-inch Bee Hummingbird of Cuba, the smallest warm- blooded creature in the world weighing in at a mere 1/15th of an ounce, to the Giant Hummingbird of Western South America that exceeds eight inches in length.

But as dazzling as their plumage is their artistry in flight. No other group of birds can perform the intricate aeriel maneuvers of the hummingbirds. They can hover in one place while feeding at a flower, fly straight up, backwards, and even upside down when the occasion demands! In addition, they are the only birds that exhibit a kind of instant terminal velocity. Whether from a perched or a hovering position, when they depart it is immediately at top speed. In fact, when they leave the perch they do not push off with their feet as other birds do. Their feet are too weak to do so: locomotion in hummingbirds is restricted solely to flight. They cannot walk, hop or crawl. This inability to move about on foot led the first taxonomists to place them in the Order Apodiformes, which implies "birds without feet"!

Speed in flight reaches a maximum of 50 to 60 miles per hour for the most rapid flyers. Their wings are just a blur; in courtship flights some species may beat their wings a remarkable 200 times per second! Normal flight, however, requires a wingbeat of some 20 to 25 beats per second. In contrast, the much larger Black-capped Chickadee beats its wings 30 times per second. It is the bird's diminutive size that deceives one into believing that the hummingbird is beating its wings much more rapidly. These wingbeats are also an example of conservation of energy. Unlike the Chickadee, which only gets power in the downstroke, the hummingbird gets power in both the up and the down stroke making the 25 beats per second much more efficient, in effect approaching 50 strokes per second.

With this much energy being expended, one would expect obtaining food to fuel these activities would be a full time job, and it is. It has been calculated that to maintain the metabolic rate of a hummingbird a person weighing 160 pounds would need to consume over 300 pounds of food per day; his metabolic rate would be so high he would become incandescent and burn up!

Food comes from two main sources: nectar from plants, and insects. The flower/hummingbird evolutionary relationship has been well studied. It shows that hummingbirds and flowers co-evolved and that the shape of flowering structures and bill-shape of hummingbirds are very specific. An example is the remarkable bill of the White-tipped Sicklebill of South America, curved to facilitate feeding in specific flowers of one wild banana. Plants have evolved strategically placed pollen sites to ensure pollination by hummingbirds visiting their flowers.

It comes as a surprise to many birders that the hummingbird diet also includes insects. These insects are often so tiny as to be difficult to be seen by the naked eye. A hummingbird flying about in a woodland or jungle glade often appears to be displaying on a territory, but close observation reveals that it is instead snapping up these tiny insects as efficiently as any flycatcher.

As with body size, bill length also varies enormously. The nearly four-inch bill of the Swordbill is longer than the rest of the bird's body, while the miniscule ⁵⁄₁₆th of an inch bill of the Purple-throated Thornbill of the High Andes is an adaptation to extreme cold.

A usually high metabolic rate and consequently the tremendous need for food lead to yet another unusual hummingbird adaptation. This is torpor. Torpor is the lowering of the body's metabolic rate overnight, when food is not readily obtainable. This lowering of metabolic rate lessens the demand for food and also allows the hummingbird to make it through exceptionally cold periods. Torpor usually occurs when the outside temperature falls to 15 degrees below the bird's normal body temperature (103 to 108 degrees according to species). While in a state of torpor the birds appear to be almost dead as they cling to their perch: when in this condition they should never be disturbed.

Hummingbird nests are marvels of engineering: constructed mainly of plant fibers and cobwebs, they are camouflaged with various plant materials such as lichens and mosses. The female does all of the building and raising of the young. During this period the males are off in their own territory or congregating in lekking sites. Lekking is a display performed by many males in a small area to attract females. In the temperate areas, males reside on individual territories by themselves. While the males are off attracting more females, the nesting female continues to set up house. Their nests take on a wide variety of forms. Some are simply cups placed in the crotch of a shrub or suspended from a limb, others are architectural wonders. Some are tiny woven baskets clasping the undersides of leaves. The nest of the Venezuelan Sooty Capped Hermit is unique: suspended from a support by a single woven mass of cobwebs, the nest bowl is off to one side of this supporting strand. If nest construction ended there, the nest would be lopsided and the eggs would fall out! However, the hummer weaves into the back side of the nest and directly below the supporting strand tiny clay balls which act as a counterweight, rectifying the nest tilt and bringing it back to level. An extraordinary feat of design and engineering!

Two eggs are usually laid, roughly ½ by ⅓ of an inch or less in size. Upon hatching, the young will remain in the nest for a month before fledging and then the female will remain attentive to them for as long as another month.

Hummingbirds are bold defenders of the nest site. I have on many occasions seen the female bombard a predator many times her size. She will fearlessly harass a hawk whose head is often larger than her whole body. No adversary seems too daunting. Cats, tree-climbing snakes and at times even people may have the wrath of a protective female hummer visited upon them.

Despite their speed and agility, danger always lurks for hummingbirds. On two occasions I have found hummingbirds caught in spider webs, obviously ensnared while obtaining silk for their nest. Other dangers include frogs and fish that leap and capture the birds as they come to drink or bathe. One eyewitness account details a fatal encounter for a tiny bird as he hovered to drink nectar, with a preying mantis hiding in the flower head!

The spectacular photos on the following pages, some of the finest ever taken, capture not only the vitality, fragility and unsurpassed beauty of the hummingbird, but also its tenacity and courage.

STREAMERTAIL

. . . .

Some have feathers of Persian lilac,
Some are wrongly called birds:
They are instead
The blossom on a flower bed.

. . . .

BORIS PASTERNAK

Copper-rumped Hummingbird

. . . .

VIOLET-TAILED SYLPH (FEMALE)
. . . .

Birds are flowers flying
and flowers perched birds.
. . . .

A. R. AMMONS

BAHAMA WOODSTAR

. . . .

. . . I thought the hummingbirds were angels
In a world of morning
And flowers
Soon invisible . . .

. . . But my eye
Prejudiced to angelic vision,

Saw them not as brown,
Which they were, brown machines;
They riffle and rifle the flowers,
Sense-drenched in September . . .

. . . .

RICHARD EBERHART

ALLEN'S HUMMINGBIRD

. . . .

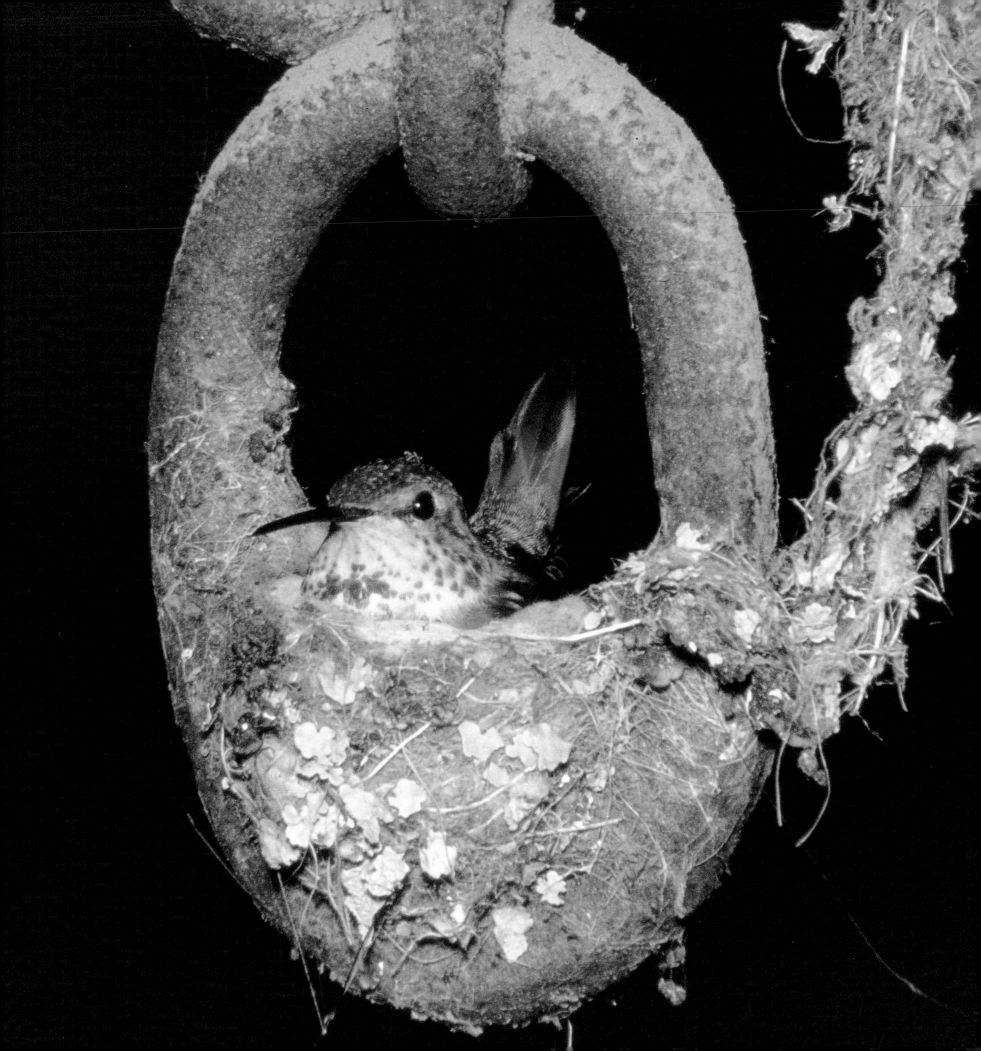

WHITE-TAILED GOLDENTHROAT
. . . .

CRIMSON TOPAZ

. . . .

WHITE-TAILED STARFRONTLET

. . . .

*Its great advantage is that it can change flight direction
at such rapid speeds, and has a sharply pointed beak to
serve as a weapon. They exploit these abilities for attack
rather than defence. Humming birds, as a rule, are
unsociable, extremely intolerant, and very
quarrelsome birds.*

. . . .

H. O. WAGNER

BLACK JACOBIN

. . . .

Rufous Hummingbird

. . . .

. . . rum explodes in the blood stream
the humming bird dreams of the thickening horn of
the hornet
sing dance drum limbo

. . . .

EDWARD KAMAN BRAITHWAITE

BROAD-TAILED HUMMINGBIRD
. . . .

How did the humming bird get its brilliant plumage?
The Kraho Indians (of Brazil) say that it was an
inquisitive bird and wanted to see what was behind the
sun. It passed right through the burning disc and took
on all the colours it found there. To this day, they say,
the humming bird is the only bird that can fly
through fire.

. . . .

AMAZONIAN MYTH

AMETHYST WOODSTAR

. . . .

Man, he sure is showin' proud
Lookin' like tiger yiye in na sun
Wid his sword held high
He gonna tak yall on . . .

. . . .

CLINTON BOY JACKSON

SWALLOW-TAILED HUMMINGBIRD

. . . .

Metallic apparition whirring
like a helicopter,
the golden nightingale of the Chinese
emperor breaking the sound
barrier, you seem almost
a weapon, too exquisite,
too expensive to be
useful, flashing
like a jewelled signal.
You could be a miniature
spacecraft from the Vegan
system.

. . . .

MARGE PIERCY

FRILLED COQUETTE

. . . .

*They fly furiously upon any intruder in their territory
and use their beaks as daggers. Not only do they attack
other humming-birds; they also attack larger birds and
even predators.*

. . . .

H. O. WAGNER

Tyrian Metaltail

I remember Blue Mountain mists
and chickens in the yard, dogs in the sun,
humming-birds flashing in the leaves,
good food and talkin' when the work is done.

MILTON REED

BLUE-THROATED HUMMINGBIRD

GREEN-TAILED TRAINBEARER

. . . .

All day long I heard the kiskidees
Lullilooing in the sun-stroked trees,
And termagant corn-birds with their raucous cries
Held in my guava tree their high assize.
The hummingbirds were busy with the flowers
And roses bloomed from recent showers.

. . . .

A. H. MENDES

BROAD-TAILED HUMMINGBIRD

. . . .

Here all beautifully collides
Unfrictioned;
Summer heals all with an oiled and motioned ease.
Here no disease . . .

. . . Here health of world in distilled proportion,
Here gyroscope ahum kept spun by bees
Who drowse-drawn lusciously entrapped by flowers
Or hummingbirds which fatten forth the hours with pure
dripped sound . . .

. . . .

RAY BRADBURY

REDDISH HERMIT

. . . .

*Hung among the flowers, in such a position that I could
see it from where I lay in bed, was a hummingbird's
nest, a tiny cup the size of half a walnut shell,
containing two pea-size white eggs. I watched the female
hummingbird sitting quietly on her eggs, while her mate
hovered and flipped among the blue flowers, like a
microscopic, glittering comet.*

. . . .

GERALD DURRELL

46

STEELY-VENTED EMERALD

. . . .

BROAD-BILLED HUMMINGBIRD

. . . .

. . . Then I watch you at the orange-
salmon faces of the canna
and you are avid.
Your long beak darts,
pokes, stabs and stabs
deep in the flesh
of the flower as you sip
hovering, standing still
in the middle of the air . . .

. . . .

MARGE PIERCY

RUBY-THROATED HUMMINGBIRD
. . . .

Whirring its wings, it was stopped before the nest, about one and a half metres in front of me, and was plucking moss from the walls. As long as one does not move, hummingbirds are not aware of a person as being something unusual, and will even examine the folds of one's clothes with bill and tongue. One hummingbird once examined the inside of my ear quite thoroughly.
. . . .

H. O. WAGNER

ANNA'S HUMMINGBIRD

. . . .

Two hummingbirds as evanescent as
Themselves
Startled me at my study window
As sea bells

Heard slipping through the fog,
Or yells
Of children down the block.

. . . .

RICHARD EBERHART

BUFF-WINGED STARFRONTLET

. . . .

A Route of Evanescence
With a revolving Wheel
A Resonance of Emerald
A Rush of Cochineal

. . . .

EMILY DICKINSON

PURPLE-BACKED THORNBILL

. . . .

LONG-TAILED WOODNYMPH

. . . .

SPECKLED HUMMINGBIRD

. . . .

Impatient, you waste no time
in going but materialize
before the bee balm, then
fast as a spark shot
from the heart of a fire
you at once thirty feet
distant drink at the phlox.

. . . .

MARGE PIERCY

BLACK-THROATED MANGO

. . . .

ANDEAN HILLSTAR

. . . .

Keen at your pleasures
you zip through the garden.
Like seeing a falling
star from the corner
of my eye, as I question
the sight, it's gone.

. . . .

MARGE PIERCY

Sparkling Violet-Ear

. . . .

Blue-tailed Hummingbird

. . . .

Colorful Puffleg

. . . .

Small, round and smooth
Burke's three categories for the beautiful,
Held in an instant . . .

. . . .

RICHARD EBERHART

GREEN-BREASTED MANGO
. . . .

Remember that the most beautiful things in the world
are the most useless . . . The purest and most thoughtful
minds are those which love colour the most.
. . . .

JOHN RUSKIN

PURPLE-THROATED
MOUNTAIN GEM

. . . .

Black-chinned Hummingbird

. . . .

Baby at every breast,
your clean greed dazzles.
Passion has streamlined you,
no waste, no hesitation.
Every dawn hones your hunger gleaming sharp
till death seizes
and drinks you down.

. . . .

MARGE PIERCY